EXTREME BUILDERS

BLACKBIRCH PRESS

An imprint of Thomson Gale, a part of The Thomson Corporation

THOMSON

GALE

Detroit • New York • San Francisco • San Diego • New Haven, Conn. • Waterville, Maine • London • Munich

© 2004 by Blackbirch Press™. Blackbirch Press™ is an imprint of The Gale Group, Inc., a division of Thomson Learning, Inc.

Blackbirch Press™ and Thomson Learning™ are trademarks used herein under license.

For more information, contact
The Gale Group, Inc.
27500 Drake Rd.
Farmington Hills, MI 48331-3535
Or you can visit our Internet site at http://www.gale.com

Photo credits: cover: Photos.com, Corel Corporation, CORBIS; all pages © Discovery Communications, Inc. except for pages 4, 12, 40 © CORBIS; pages 8, 24, 38 © Corel Corporation; pages 16, 20, 28, 30, 32, 34, 44 © Photos.com

LIBRARY OF CONGRESS CATALOGING-IN-PUBLICATION DATA

Extreme Builders / Marla Felkins Ryan, book editor.
  p. cm. — (Planet's most extreme)
  Includes bibliographical references and index.
  ISBN 1-4103-0384-5 (hard cover : alk. paper)
    1-4103-0426-4 (paper cover : alk. paper)
  1. Animals—Shelter—Juvenile literature. 2. Shelter—Juvenile literature. I. Ryan, Marla Felkins II. Title. III. Series.

Printed in China
10 9 8 7 6 5 4 3 2 1

Our buildings may be skyscrapers, but when it comes to construction, the real high-rises can be found in the animal kingdom. We're counting down the top ten most extreme animal architects and comparing them with human attempts to build their way into the record books. Discover that you'll need more than concrete and steel to take building to The Most Extreme.

10

The African
Grey Tree Frog

At number ten in the countdown are animals with a problem.
Frogs need to keep their eggs moist and safe from hungry eyes.
Some frogs take their chances hiding their eggs on the forest
floor. One frog, though, has a passion for building.

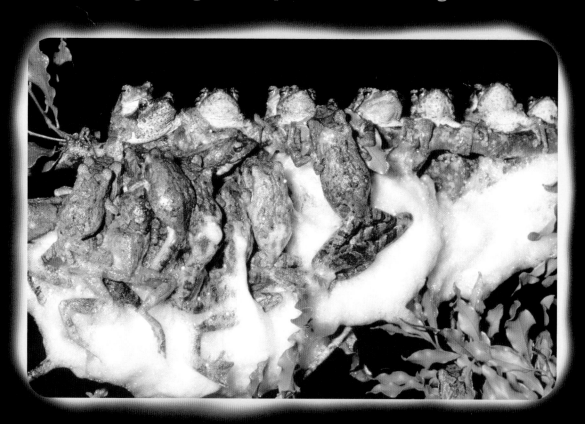

Hopping in at number ten, the African grey tree frog has a real passion for building.

For these African grey tree frogs, mating is a messy business. That's because the frogs build as they breed. The female secretes a foamy fluid from her skin when she releases her eggs for the males to fertilize. Then everybody kicks in to beat the babies' home into shape. This extreme team is number ten in the countdown because these bubbles set like concrete to provide a foam home against all kinds of weather.

Our earliest ancestors also had a passion for building. Once they got the hang of fire, they developed other tools that let them move

Humans' passion for building has enabled us to build shelters on earth and in outer space!

out of natural shelters and into man-made caves. Safe inside our modern homes, we've managed to almost completely seal ourselves away from nature. Our buildings provide the warmth, safety, and shelter we need to survive in even the most extreme environments—both on (and off) the planet.

State-of-the-art building technology has taken us out of this world, but just like the astronauts, the time the grey tree frog spends hanging in space is only temporary. After a few weeks, the bubble house starts to dissolve, and the tadpoles discover that the real-estate business is all about location, location, location. Tree frogs always build their foam homes over water, so their babies can drop into the pond where they swim away to start their new life.

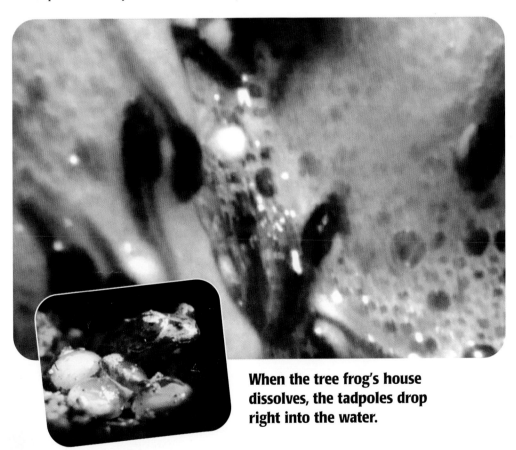

When the tree frog's house dissolves, the tadpoles drop right into the water.

The
Oranguntan

There's one big difference separating us from other builders in the animal kingdom. We use tools to help us. Take a close look at the great apes, though, and you'll discover that when it comes to building, gorillas, orangutans and chimps are definitely not chumps.

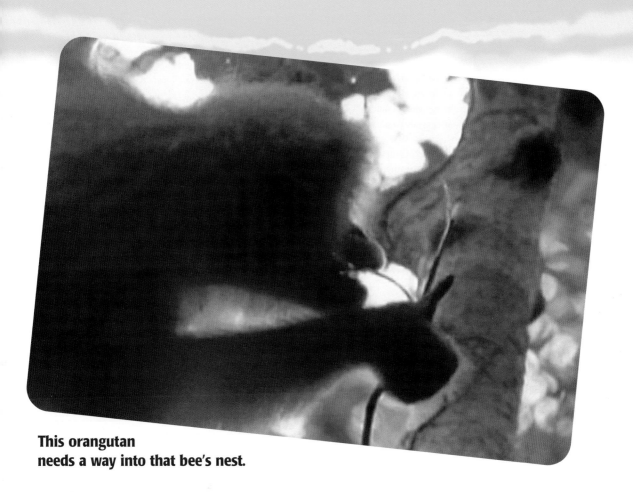

**This orangutan
needs a way into that bee's nest.**

A honey-extraction tool does the trick!

This orang has a problem. She's found a bee's nest, but the honey is out of reach of even her long fingers. The solution? Build a honey extraction tool.

Very few animals have the ability to make even this simple tool. But the ape's intelligence isn't the reason that orangutans are number nine in the countdown. For this is the face of a master builder—and the thing orangs build best are beds.

Orangutans and other apes are highly intelligent.

They're the best bed builders in the world.

At the end of each day, high in the forest canopy, orangutans retire to a new tree to weave a new bed. Because they're constantly moving through the forest, orangs really do have to make their bed every day. That's up to 15,000 beds in a lifetime!

Luckily for us, these great apes seem content being the best bed builders in the world. For just imagine how our lives could change if apes started building with the right tools!

8 The **Bowerbird**

What makes a luxury home? It's a matter of combining quality construction with beautiful interior design. That's why coming in at number eight in the countdown is the best builder of luxury love shacks in the world.

This bowerbird has built quite a love shack.

Meet the male bowerbird. Back in 1872, the first naturalist to see the incredible constructions of this extreme builder thought they must be built by humans. Surely no bird could weave such a structure and decorate it with such artistic precision! But it's amazing what a male will do for a mate.

There are 19 species of bowerbirds in Australia and New Guinea, and they all have different ways of impressing the girls with their home handyman skills. This is a satin bowerbird nicknamed Jock. He's famous for his efforts to create the best bower in the district. Jock knows his girlfriends only have one favorite color, so he travels far and wide to collect absolutely anything so long as it's blue.

Jock, though, is no match for the Vogelkop bowerbird, who builds a hut that's up to six feet wide and four feet high! He also tends pretty flowers in a garden and replaces them as soon as they fade. Males also collect pretty trinkets like beetle wing covers, feathers, fungi, and even one naturalist's pair of brightly colored socks!

Even bowerbirds can't compete with the eccentric creations of some human males. How would you like to live in a house made of lots of empty bottles? Lots of empty bottles of embalming fluid? This house in Red Deer, Alberta, is the dream home of retired undertaker David Brown. He had always wanted to build his own house, and he decided that the square-shaped embalming bottles would be the ideal construction material. By the time the house was finished, he had cemented into the walls an incredible 600,000 bottles!

Meanwhile, in Houston, Texas, there's a house made out of a very different building material. John Milkovisch was a man who liked beer. He liked beer a lot. Every day for 18 years, he drained a six-pack and incorporated the cans into his house. With the enthusiastic help of friends and neighbors, John emptied a staggering 39,000 cans!

Like John, the sociable weaverbird relies on a little help from its friends to build the most extreme nest on the planet. On the plains of Africa, these birds create enormous nests high in trees. Weighing more than a ton, this apartment block can house more than 400 birds!

One of these incredible nests has been in use for more than 100 years—which is more than can be said for our first attempts at apartment living two thousand years ago. Once all roads really did lead to Rome, so city planners had to find a way to house all the people flocking to the city. Luckily, the Romans had just discovered

The weaverbirds in Africa that constructed this enormous nest are extreme builders.

concrete, so they were able to copy the weaverbirds and build multistoried apartments. Unfortunately, they hadn't discovered reinforcing, which limited the height they could build safely.

Today, thanks to reinforced concrete and steel technology, we can build superstructures more than twenty times taller than the apartments of ancient Rome. And buildings don't get much taller than the Petronas Towers in Kuala Lumpur, Malaysia. Each tower is supported by an outer ring of 16 concrete columns that push the building more than 1,400 feet into the sky. It took 7,000 people five years to complete the Petronas Towers. But could any of them compete with the sociable weaverbird, and make a house of hay that would last for 100 years?

7 The **Spider**

Some of the most delicate structures in nature can also be the deadliest. That's why coming in at number seven in the countdown is the spider. All spiders build with silk they produce from glands in their bottom. Silk starts as a liquid, but quickly hardens into a thread that can be spun into that deadly web.

By building their web across busy air space, spiders can filter food from the sky. A web of spider's silk is no ordinary fishing net, though. That's because you need a very special building material to capture high-speed insects. To keep bugs from bouncing off, spiders cover their webs with glue.

Looks like this insect won't be flying anywhere else.

Why doesn't the spider get caught in its own web? Take a close look at the silk strands and you'll see distinct blobs of glue. By picking its way between the blobs, the spider can move freely across the web.

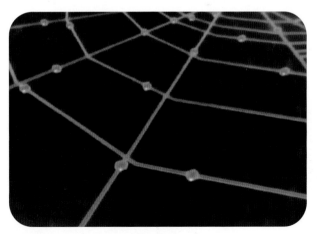

Spiders step between these blobs of glue so they never get stuck in their webs.

And webs have to be strong. This tropical orb-weaving spider makes the biggest and strongest web on the planet. A single web can be more than six feet across. Silk lines can run 30 feet up into the trees and are strong enough to catch small birds!

Spider silk is an amazing building material. Weight for weight, spider silk is twice as elastic as nylon and five times stronger than steel. No wonder spiders can build structures to rival those of any human engineer. Imagine how different our constructions would be if we could use a material that could hold 4,000 times its own weight and be anchored with nothing but glue.

The average garden spider makes enough silk in its lifetime to stretch three times across the Brooklyn Bridge! Spiderwebs are also environmentally friendly. How many human engineers could recycle their creations by eating them?

This Peruvian pink toe spider can spin an entire tent out of silk.

Spiders are most famous for spinning silk into their deadly webs. But they have also found other uses for their versatile silk, as Jane Stevens from the St. Louis Zoo explains:

"Not all spiders weave webs to catch food. This is a Peruvian pink toe. She makes a wonderful tent out of silk. She lives in the rain forest, but she can live in many other habitats because that silk tent gives her lots of humidity. If it gets too dry she can always retreat into her silken tent to get the humidity that she needs."

**When they hatch,
baby spiders can eat their silk home.**

From the moment they're born, spiders make use of silk.
Their eggs are wrapped in a silk case, which can become a
nourishing first meal. Then, depending on the kind of spider,
silk can be used to build homes, wrap up food, and even to
travel!

Small spiders can build themselves a parachute. A single
thread of silk is light enough to be picked up by the wind,
and strong enough to carry the spiderling. So it's up, up, and
away. Although sometimes cruising at 30,000 feet can be
dangerous!

6

The **Prairie Dog**

This fat little rodent doesn't look like your average city slicker, but it's number six in the countdown because it builds the best little house on the prairie. These are prairie dogs, and each one of those mounds is the top of a house.

At number six in our countdown, prairie dogs are extreme tunnelers.

In a prairie dog town, there are a lot of houses packed as tightly as any suburb. It's just that to see prairie dog buildings at their best, you have to head underground.

That's because prairie dogs take tunneling to the extreme. Combine all the tunnels of all the dogs living under the prairie and you end up with an underground metropolis. Especially when you consider how many dogs once used to build their homes in America. One prairie dog town in Texas was estimated to have a population of 400 million dogs!

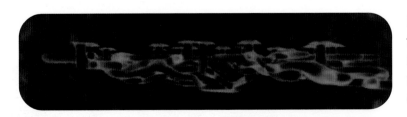

Prairie dog tunnels make up entire underground cities.

Some humans also spend a lot of time underground. Unlike prairie dogs, they use a massive machine to build their tunnels for them. This is one of the most powerful hard rock boring machines ever built. It can grind its way through more than 60 feet of solid rock each day. It weighs more than 900 tons and needs a crew of 25 just to keep it running. It really is an extreme machine. Yet prairie dogs manage to build their vast tunnels with nothing but their bare hands.

These builders use their bare hands to make their underground homes.

Digging a burrow complete with bedrooms, bathrooms, and nurseries means the prairie dog is left with an awful lot of dirt back on the surface. Yet even this can be built into a useful

The dirt mounds they create are useful lookout points.

mound. In these flat grasslands, flooding can be a real problem, unless you a build protective dikes of dirt. And these raised mounds also make a useful lookout points, for there are many dangers on the prairie.

When a prairie dog dives into its burrow, nothing short of a giant vacuum cleaner would get it out again. And in Utah, that's just what they've got! This souped-up sewage truck sucks up prairie dogs! It may not be the most dignified way to be relocated, but at least the dogs are going to a place where they will be safer from human activities.

Let's suck up some prairie dogs.

X 5

The Caddisfly

The prairie dog may have laid the foundations for our countdown to find the most extreme builder on the planet, but next is animal whose house is a work of art.

It's winter in West Virginia, and Kathy Stout is on the trail of number five in our countdown of extreme builders. Take a close look at the leaves in this stream and you'll find that our builder has been at work. These circular holes mean that our animal is going to be hard to see.

The pieces missing from this leaf have gone to good use.

The missing leaf pieces are now the home of the caddisfly. Caddisfly larvae are number five in the countdown because they can build a house out of anything.

A caddisfly used them as building material.

These extreme builders are mostly harmless vegetarians, so they need a way of avoiding hungry eyes. That's why they'll build a home that's camouflaged to look like just another part of the streambed. And if the construction material is too big, their powerful jaws will soon cut it into the right shape. Then they use their spit as a glue! Modified salivary glands make a kind of silk to bind the pieces together.

**Pieces of leaf bound
with gluelike spit are
perfect camouflage.**

Caddisflies will stick anything together to make their mobile
homes. Sometimes caddisflies are such masters of disguise
that their houses can fool other hungry herbivores, but caddisflies can't fool Kathy Stout. Kathy is in the business of
changing caddisflies from builders to jewelers. She explains:

> In our labs we've constructed our own simulated stream. We've
> been able to find beautiful types of stones to get the caddisflies
> to work with. We give them lapis, and so forth. I just look at the
> color of the stones I like and I say, "Let's crush that one or crush
> this one," and then we crush them to simulate the same size
> stones they would normally pick up in the stream.

It's just that the stones you find in the stream are a little drab compared to these works of art. With a little skill, caddisfly cases become truly unique beads that can be worked into some of nature's finest jewelry. Don't worry about the flies though. Kathy says,

The bead on this chain was once a caddisfly's home.

> *There are no caddisflies harmed in the making of our jewelry. We raise the caddisfly until it's an adult and then we let our little guys go.*

That's because even the most beautiful construction in the countdown is no use to an adult caddisfly. Once they leave the water, adults only have one thing on their mind, and it isn't building or eating. Some caddisflies only live for a few days, so the race is on to find a mate and start making the next generation of extreme jewelers.

Caddisfly cases are some of nature's finest jewelry.

The Nautilus

It's a high-pressure business trying to build a home deep under water. That's because for every 100 feet you descend, another 45 pounds of force presses in against you. One animal, though, makes it look easy. At number four in the countdown is the nautilus.

This mollusk normally spends the day 1,000 feet below the waves. Haul some deep-sea fish to the surface and the change in pressure could be lethal, but this is a journey the nautilus makes every night. It moves up to hunt in shallow waters, chasing down its prey using a form of jet propulsion, just like its cousin the squid. When the sun rises, the nautilus sinks.

The nautilus can survive these extreme pressure changes, thanks to its incredible shell. This structure is a truly stunning piece of design, according to Dr. Bruce Carlson from Hawaii's Waikiki Aquarium. He explains:

The nautilus starts its life in a tiny shell that grows with it.

When the chambered nautilus hatches it's a miniature of the adult, it has a very tiny shell like this, and obviously it has to grow as the animal increases in size. To see how it does that, let's look inside the nautilus's shell. The animal actually occupies this part of the shell, and as it grows it forms a new chamber here, a septum. That forms a new chamber, and as it continues to grow it'll move forward and create a new chamber, till about the time it's an adult it'll have thirty chambers. Now at the same time it's also adding shell at the lip, so that it increases in size throughout its life.

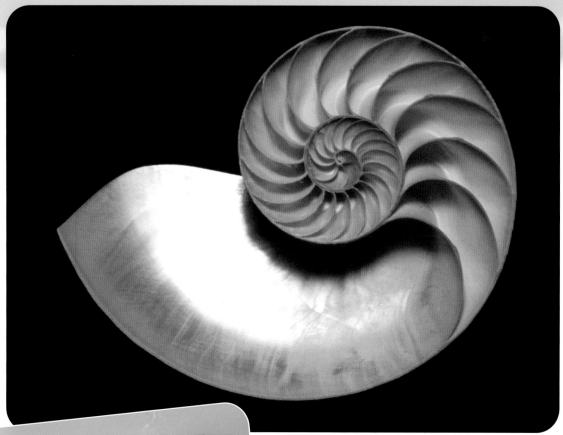

By secreting calcium carbonate, the nautilus adds chamber after chamber to its shell.

The nautilus is number four in the countdown because simply by secreting calcium carbonate, it can build a shell that lets it travel across the vast depths of the ocean. It's no wonder that the nineteenth-century science-fiction writer Jules Verne looked to this mollusk for inspiration. He named his fantastic deep-sea submersible the *Nautilus* in his classic adventure, *Twenty Thousand Leagues Under the Sea*. Carlson explains why this name was appropriate:

The nautilus probably has its closest relation in our world to the submarine. Like the submarine, the nautilus animal is able to move deeper and deeper and able to withstand external pressure. But there is a maximum depth, and when the nautilus gets to about 1,500 feet, the shell will implode. Still, when you think about the fact it can go from 0 to 1,500 ft with a shell that's only about one millimeter thick, it's a very remarkable animal in that regard.

To show just how remarkable, imagine what would happen to a human head at such extreme depths. (This head's actually polystyrene, because nobody could hold their breath for the length of time it takes a submersible to descend to the depths of the nautilus). The immense pressure squeezes the polystyrene until it's less than half its original size!

Humans need a submarine to reach the depths the nautilus does.

Although Jules Verne wrote about his incredible submarine back in 1870, it took well into the next century for us to build machines that could dive to the depths of the real nautilus. Modern science-fiction writers still dream of building homes beneath the waves, but for the moment, this alien world belongs to the nautilus.

3

The Bee

Coming in at number three in the countdown is a true believer in flower power. The bee is an extreme engineer that harvests flowers for raw materials. For bees turn nectar and pollen into wax, and wax is an extraordinary building material.

More than 50,000 extreme builders call this nest their home.

A large nest like this can weigh several hundred pounds and house more than 50,000 bees. And it's built of nothing but wax. Inside the nest are the rows of hexagonal cells that Charles Darwin described as a "masterpiece of engineering." The cells are used to store food—which is why we call it "honeycomb." A typical colony stores away 40 pounds of honey to survive the winter. The cells of wax are also the nursery for the thousands of grubs that are raised each year.

A typical nest is made from about two and a half pounds of beeswax. To find out where all this wax comes from you need to take a close look at a bee's bottom. For between the segments of the abdomen are glands that produce the wax that bees use to build. It's not easy, though.

The bees only produce tiny flakes of wax, no bigger than a pinhead. It takes half a million flakes to make one pound of beeswax. And every one of those flakes has to be carefully molded into the walls of the hexagonal cells, all 100,000 of them.

Bees skillfully mold each wax flake into these hexagonal shapes.

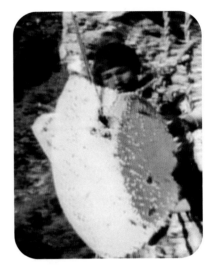

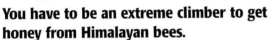
You have to be an extreme climber to get honey from Himalayan bees.

Thanks to the honey stored in all those cells, bees are definitely our favorite builders. We even help them by providing artificial tree trunks for them to live in. Today we build wooden hives with movable frames, but in the past, beekeepers would use conical baskets woven from straw or cane.

To be a beekeeper in the Himalayas, you have to have a head for heights. For these bees build their nests in such extreme positions that Nepalese honey hunters are pushed right to the edge. If you think these builders make life uncomfortable, just wait until you meet the next contender, who's also got a reputation for being difficult.

The **Beaver**

When it comes to building big, nothing beats a dam. And in nature, when it comes to dams, nothing builds better than number two in our countdown.

Beavers use their teeth and paws to build the best dams in nature.

The beaver has been building dams for five million years. With nothing but teeth and paws, it can create a 1,000-foot long structure sturdy enough to support a family car.

Beavers build because they love water. They get protection by placing their home in the middle of their artificial lake. The lodge is like a castle surrounded by a moat. And the moat is also the beaver's garden, full of its favorite food. Only one animal has a more dramatic impact on its environment—and we don't build with our teeth.

No tree is safe when a beaver decides to start building.

Since the first large-scale dam was built in Egypt 5,000 years ago, human engineers have been busy little beavers, constantly devising new ways of taming the forces of raging rivers. The biggest challenge of them all will be in China, where people aim to dam the third largest river in the world.

Here on the Yangtze River, the Three Gorges dam will become the world's biggest hydroelectric dam. More than 1 million people will lose their homes when these valleys are flooded. The beaver is also capable of a little destruction. No tree is safe from this rodent's terrible teeth. It can chew through a log the size of a rolling pin in only 15 seconds! With teeth as sharp as chisels, a family of these furry chainsaws can fell several hundred trees and saplings in the course of a single winter.

Cutting down trees is the easy part. If we wanted to build a dam like a beaver, we'd have to develop some other special skills, as animal educator David Kleven explains:

Humans have a lot of catching up to do to build dams like beavers do.

You could call beavers the tug-boats of the water world because of their incredible swimming abili-ty. They can pull very large logs through the water. They actually have 4 sets of lips so they can carry something in their mouth with their teeth and keep from swallowing water. Many people believe that the flat tail of the beaver is used for pushing and propelling them through water, but actually the tail is used more as a rudder, as a steering mechanism, than as an actual propulsion tool.

But even the beaver is no match for the ultimate builder on the planet.

The beaver uses its tail as a rudder to steer itself through the water.

1

The **Termite**

To find the most extreme buildings, you just have to travel to any big city on the planet. We like to build skyscrapers— enormous monuments to our power and wealth. One creature, though, builds on an even bigger scale.

**Our countdown's
number one builder has made
the Empire State Building of the animal kingdom.**

It's easy to be impressed by the Empire State Building and its 102 floors. Yet if the number one animal in the countdown were the same size as a human—scaled up to our size—it would make a skyscraper four times the size of the Empire State Building! The building would be empty, though, because these builders live in the basement—all 5 million of them.

The Empire State Building of the animal kingdom is found on the plains of Africa. Standing 20 feet tall, this mighty tower is home to the number one builder in the countdown. It's just that they're all busy down in the basement.

The most extreme builders on the planet are termites!
What they lack in size they make up for in sheer numbers.

The enormous queen can give birth every 15 seconds, so
there's no shortage of workers to help construct their massive
home. And they need all the help they can get, because for

**Termites may be small, but they are
the most extreme builders on earth.**

The queen termite is enormous and can give birth every 15 seconds!

termites, building is a very messy business. That's because the entire termite tower is made from a mixture of saliva, dirt, and dung. And they have to mix it all together in their mouths.

Termites mix saliva, dirt, and dung to make their building material.

It may not be pretty, but this plaster sets like concrete and can be molded into extraordinary design features like air conditioning systems, covered walkways, stairs, and gardens. There's not a single window, though, because termites are blind.

Ancient Egyptians invented a strong building material for their pyramids . . . concrete.

In Egypt there are also huge, windowless buildings. But at least the workers who made the pyramids didn't have to chew mouthfuls of dirt and dung. Instead, they invented the first form of concrete, which has survived for more than 4,000 years!

It only took 30 years to build the Great Pyramid, yet it remained the tallest building on earth until 1889! It's hard to imagine that a building that towers over the Statue of Liberty could be made from blocks of solid stone! The blocks weigh about two tons, and there are more than two and a half million in the pyramid! With our modern building techniques, that's enough stone to make more than 40 Empire State Buildings!

Termites may not build out of solid stone, but their constructions are just as impressive. For even though it's held together by nothing more than spit and poop, the termite mound can endure for more than one hundred years. So it's no wonder, that when it comes to building, termites really are the Most Extreme.

**Termites . . .
our planet's Most Extreme!**

For More Information

Stephen Brend, *Orangutan.* Austin, TX: Raintree Steck-Vaughn, 2000.

Margery Facklam, *What's the Buzz? The Secret Life of Bees.* Austin, TX : Raintree Steck-Vaughn, 2001.

Jen Green, *Prairie Dogs.* Danbury, CT: Grolier, 2001.

Janet Halfmann, *The Tallest Building.* San Diego: KidHaven, 2004.

Lee Jacobs, *Beaver.* San Diego: Blackbirch, 2003.

Marybeth Lorbiecki, *Prairie Dogs.* Chanhassen, MN: NorthWord Press, 2004.

Patricia A. Fink Martin, *Orangutans.* New York: Children's Press, 2000.

Darlyne Murawski, *Spiders and Their Webs.* Washington, DC: National Geographic Society, 2004.

Catherine Petrini, *The Petronas Towers.* San Diego: Blackbirch, 2004.

Ann O. Squire, *Termites.* Danbury, CT: Children's Press, 2003.

Glossary

abdomen: One of the three segments of an insect's body.

conical: Cone shaped.

dike: A bank of earth built to prevent flooding.

eccentric: Unusual; whimsical.

embalming fluid: Chemical used to prepare dead bodies for burial.

gland: An organ that removes materials from the blood and secretes them for a
different purpose.

herbivore: An animal that eats mainly plants.

hexagonal: Six sided.

lapis: Lapis lazuli, a semiprecious stone usually deep blue in color.

metropolis: Large city.

mollusk: Shellfish.

naturalist: Biologist, usually one who studies animals in their natural habitat.

polystyrene: A hard plastic.

reinforcing: Embedding metal in concrete to add strength.

salivary: Saliva producing.

secrete: To form and emit.

spiderling: Young spider.

submersible: Underwater vehicle.

Index

abdomen, 34
African grey tree frog, 4–7
apes, 8–11

beaver, 36–39
beds, 10–11
bee, 32–35
birds, 12–15
bottles, 14
bowerbird, 12–15

caddisfly, 24–27
camouflage, 25
cans, 14
concrete, 15, 44

dam, 36–39

eggs, 4, 5
Egypt, 44

foam, 5, 7
flowers, 32

frogs, 4–7

glands, 16, 25, 34
grubs, 33

honey, 33, 35
house, 14, 20–23

insects, 17

jet propulsion, 29

mating, 5, 27
mollusk, 29

nautilus, 28–31
nectar, 32
nest, 14, 33, 34

orangutan, 8–11

paws, 37
prairie dog, 20–23

pyramids, 44

rodent, 20

salivary glands, 25
shell, 29–30
silk, 16–19, 25
skyscrapers, 15, 40, 41
spider, 16–19
submarine, 31

tadpoles, 7
tail, 39
teeth, 37, 38
termite, 40–45
tree frog, 4–7
tunnels, 21, 22

vegetarian, 25

wax, 33, 34
web, 17, 18

GLOSSARY

aloof Not involved with or friendly toward other people.

assault To attack someone violently.

culmination The end or final result of something.

fundamentals The most important or basic parts of something.

mentor Someone who teaches or gives help and advice to a less experienced and often younger person.

offense The means or method of attacking or of attempting to score.

professional Paid to participate in a sport or activity.

retire To end your working or professional career.

rookie A first-year player in a professional sport.

strategy A plan or method for achieving a particular goal.

tendon Tough piece of tissue in your body that connects muscle to bone.

union An organization of workers formed to protect the rights and interests of its members.

Books

Christopher, Matt, and Glenn Stout. *On the Court with… Kobe Bryant.* New York, NY: Little, Brown Books for Young Readers, 2009.

Gitlin, Marty. *Kobe Bryant: NBA Champion.* Edina, MN: Sportzone, 2011.

Indovino, Shaina. *Kobe Bryant* (Superstars in the World of Basketball). Broomall, PA: Mason Crest, 2014.

Savage, Jeff. *Kobe Bryant.* Rev. ed. Minneapolis, MN: Lerner Publications, 2013.

Stewart, Mark. *The Los Angeles Lakers* (Team Spirit). Chicago, IL: Norwood House Press, 2014.

Thornley, Stew. *Kobe Bryant: Champion Basketball Star.* Berkeley Heights, NJ: Enslow Publishers, 2013.

Wukovits, John. *Kobe Bryant* (People in the News). San Diego, CA: Lucent Books, 2011.

Websites

Because of the changing nature of Internet links, Rosen Publishing has developed an online list of websites related to the subject of this book. This site is updated regularly. Please use this link to access the list:

http://www.rosenlinks.com/LLS/Bry

INDEX

A

After-School All-Stars, 36
All-Defensive team, NBA, 17, 19, 20, 22, 24, 25, 30
All-NBA team, 17, 19, 20, 22, 24, 25, 30, 35
All-Rookie team, NBA, 14
All-Star Games/teams, NBA, 16, 17, 19, 25, 28, 30, 32, 35

B

Boston Celtics, 25
Brown, Mike, 32, 33
Bryant, Joe, 6, 8, 12, 35
Bryant, Kobe
    and assault charges, 22
    childhood, 6–10
    with the L.A. Lakers, 4, 5, 13, 14–25, 28–35, 39, 40
    marriage and children, 37–39
    and 1996 draft, 12–13
    and the Olympics, 26
    origin of name and nick-names, 6, 17, 30
    records held/milestones, 10, 13, 14, 16, 28, 30, 32, 35

C

Chamberlain, Wilt, 5, 24, 25, 28
Charlotte Hornets, 13
Chicago Bulls, 17, 32
Cox, Chubby, 8

D

D'Antoni, Mike, 33–35
Detroit Pistons, 22
Divac, Vlade, 13

G

Gasol, Pau, 28

H

Hill, Grant, 26
Houston Rockets, 6, 35
Howard, Dwight, 35

J

Jackson, Phil, 17, 20, 22, 32, 33
Johnson, Wesley, 39
Jones, Eddie, 14
Jordan, Michael, 5, 32

K

Kobe Doin' Work, 30

L

Laine, Vanessa, 37
Lee, Spike, 30
Los Angeles Clippers, 22
Los Angeles Lakers, 4, 5, 13, 14–25, 28–35, 39, 40
Lower Merion High School, 10

M

Miami Heat, 22

N

Nash, Steve, 33–35
NBA lockouts, 17, 32
New York Knicks, 28

O

Oklahoma City Thunder, 32
Olympic Games, 26
O'Neal, Shaquille, 17–19, 20,
   22, 32
Osgood-Schlatter disease, 10

P

Phoenix Suns, 22, 25, 35
Princeton offense, 35

S

San Antonio Spurs, 17
Stockton, John, 35

T

Toronto Raptors, 24, 35
triangle offense, 17, 19

U

Utah Jazz, 16, 35

V

Van Exel, Nick, 14